This is Kate with her father. Sometimes she calls him 'Daddy' but mostly just 'Dad'.

Peter's dad was there at Peter's birth. He held his son when he was only a few minutes old.

Meet the family
My Dad

by Mary Auld

WORCESTERSHIRE
COUNTY COUNCIL

259

Bertrams   29/01/2009

J306.8742   £5.99

BV

700035402591

FRANKLIN WATTS
LONDON·SYDNEY

Serena is adopted. Her dad says they became a real family the day Serena arrived.

Claire's step-dad
is called Simon.
He lives with Claire,
her mum and her
baby brother, Kevin.

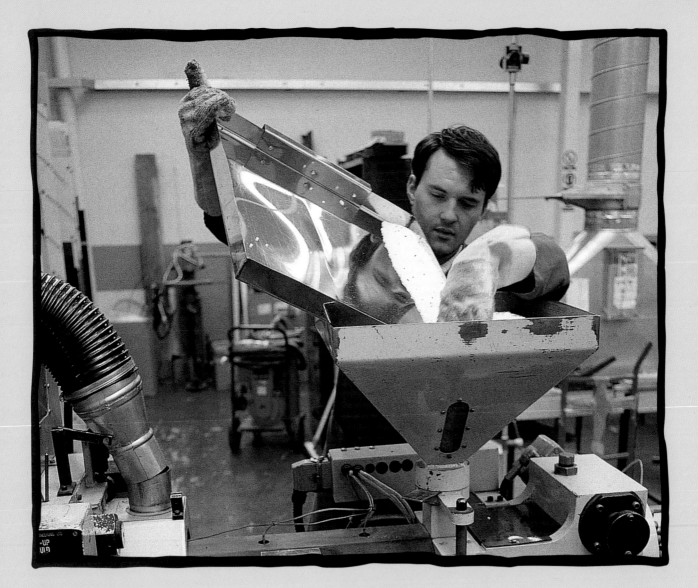

Teresa's dad
works in a factory.

Jackie's dad is
a photographer.

Brian's dad
is a farmer.

Andy's dad works from
home, so he spends a lot
of time with Andy, too.

Amanda's dad helps
her with her reading
after school.

Martin likes helping his dad to cook.

Callum likes going fishing with his dad.

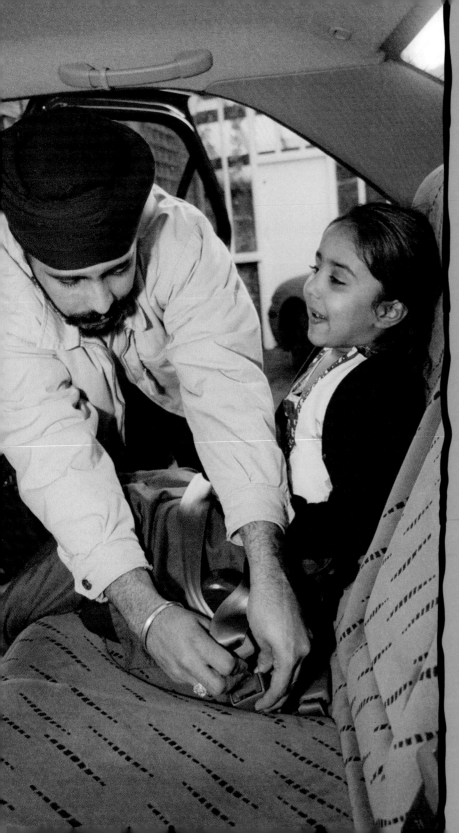

Gurpreet's dad makes sure her safety belt is fastened in the car.

Kevin's dad makes sure Kevin brushes his teeth before bedtime.

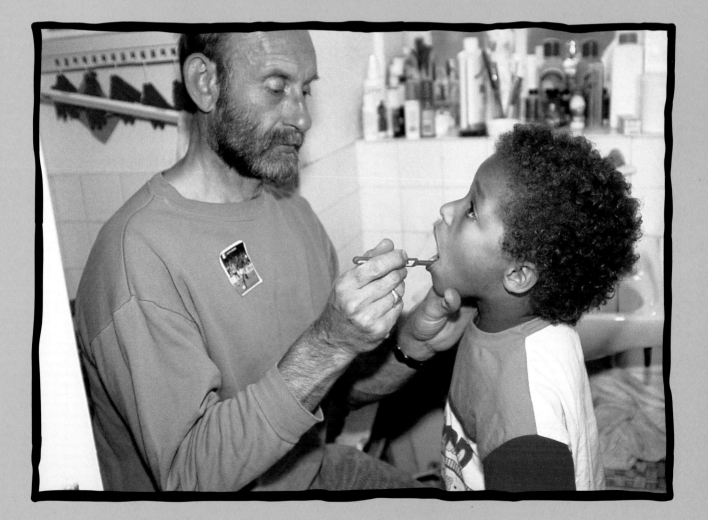

This is Sam, his dad
and his dad's dad –
Grandpa Jim.

What's your dad like?

Family words

Here are some words people use when talking about their dad or family.

Names for dad:
Father, Daddy, Dad, Pa, parent.

Names for mum:
Mother, Mummy, Mum, Ma, parent.

Names of other relatives:
Son, Daughter; Brother, Sister; Grandchildren; Grandparents; Grandmother, Granny, Grandma; Grandfather, Grandad, Grandpa; Uncle; Aunt, Auntie; Nephew, Niece.

If we put the word 'Step' in front of a relative's name it means that we are related to them by marriage but not by birth.

When people are adopted, they become part of a family by law, although they were not born into that family.

A family tree

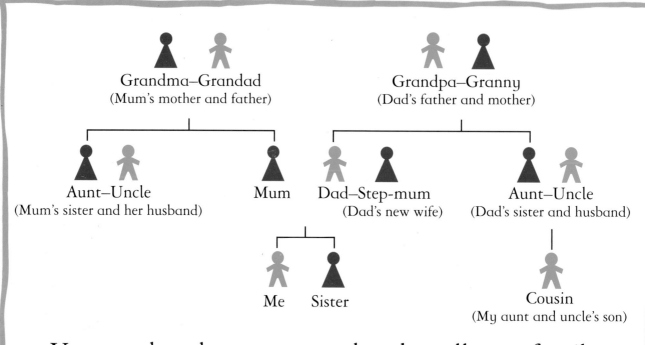

Grandma–Grandad
(Mum's mother and father)

Grandpa–Granny
(Dad's father and mother)

Aunt–Uncle
(Mum's sister and her husband)

Mum

Dad–Step-mum
(Dad's new wife)

Aunt–Uncle
(Dad's sister and husband)

Me   Sister

Cousin
(My aunt and uncle's son)

You can show how you are related to all your family
on a plan like this one. It is called a family tree.
Every family tree is different. Try drawing your own.

Published in 2008 by Franklin Watts,
338 Euston Road, London NW1 3BH

Franklin Watts Australia
Level 17/207 Kent Street, Sydney NSW 2000

Copyright © Franklin Watts 2003

Series editor: Rachel Cooke
Art director: Jonathan Hair
Design: Andrew Crowson

A CIP catalogue record for this book
is available from the British Library.

ISBN 978 0 7496 8104 3

Printed in Hong Kong/China

Acknowledgements:
Bruce Berman/Corbis: front cover centre below.
www.johnbirdsall.co.uk: front cover centre top, 2, 4,
6, 7, 8, 18. Joanne O'Brien/Format: 1, 13-14. Carlos
Goldin/Corbis: front cover centre above. Don
Gray/Photofusion: 5. Richard Greenhill, Sally &
Richard Greenhill: 10. Ronnie Kauffman/ Corbis:
20. Roy Morsch/Corbis: 17. Jose Luis Pelaez/Corbis:
front cover main, 22. Ulrike Press/Format: 11, 19.
Chuck Savage/ Corbis: 16. George Shelley/Corbis:
front cover bottom. Ariel Skelley/Corbis: front cover
centre, 12. Christa Stadtler/Photofusion: 13.

Whilst every attempt has been made to clear copyright should there be any inadvertent omission
please apply in the first instance to the publisher
regarding rectification.

Franklin Watts is a division of Hachette Children's
Books, an Hachette Livre UK company.
www.hachettelivre.co.uk

Please note that some of the pictures in this book
have been posed by models.